ALL ABOUT FALL

People in Fall

by Martha E. H. Rustad

Consulting Editor: Gail Saunders-Smith, PhD

Capstone
press

Mankato, Minnesota

Pebble Plus is published by Capstone Press,
151 Good Counsel Drive, P.O. Box 669, Mankato, Minnesota 56002.
www.capstonepress.com

1 2 3 4 5 6 12 11 10 09 08 07

Library of Congress Cataloging-in-Publication Data
Rustad, Martha E. H. (Martha Elizabeth Hillman), 1975–
People in fall / by Martha E. H. Rustad.
p. cm. —(Pebble plus. All about fall)
Summary: "Simple text and photographs present people in fall"—Provided by publisher.
Includes bibliographical references and index.
ISBN-13: 978-1-4296-0025-5 (hardcover)
ISBN-10: 1-4296-0025-X (hardcover)
1. Autumn—Juvenile literature. I. Title. II. Series.
QB637.7.R87 2008
508.2—dc22   2006102055

Editorial Credits
Sarah L. Schuette, editor; Veronica Bianchini, designer

Photo Credits
Capstone Press/Karon Dubke, all

Note to Parents and Teachers

The All about Fall set supports national science standards related to changes during
the seasons. This book describes and illustrates the people in fall. The images support
early readers in understanding the text. The repetition of words and phrases helps early
readers learn new words. This book also introduces early readers to subject-specific
vocabulary words, which are defined in the Glossary section. Early readers may need
assistance to read some words and to use the Table of Contents, Glossary, Read More,
Internet Sites, and Index sections of the book.

Table of Contents

Fall Is Here

It's fall.

The days are shorter.

The weather is colder.

4

What We Do

We wear sweaters
and jackets to play outside.

School starts in fall.

We walk to school.

We wear costumes
on Halloween.
We go trick-or-treating.

10

We celebrate Thanksgiving.
We eat turkey, potatoes,
and corn.

Getting Ready

We get ready for winter.

We harvest vegetables

from our garden.

We pick ripe apples
from trees in our yard.

We rake the fallen leaves
into piles.

Other Signs of Fall

In fall, people are busy getting ready for winter. What are other signs that it's fall?

Glossary

costume—clothes worn by people dressing up

garden—an area of dirt where flowers and vegetables are planted

Halloween—a holiday celebrated on October 31; people dress in costumes and go trick-or-treating on Halloween.

harvest—to gather crops that are ripe

ripe—ready to be harvested, picked, or eaten

Read More

Latta, Sara L. *What Happens in Fall?* I Like the Seasons! Berkeley Heights, N.J.: Enslow Elementary, 2006.

Schuette, Sarah L. *Let's Look at Fall.* Pebble Plus: Investigate the Seasons. Mankato, Minn.: Capstone Press, 2007.

Internet Sites

FactHound offers a safe, fun way to find Internet sites related to this book. All of the sites on FactHound have been researched by our staff.

Here's how:

1. Visit *www.facthound.com*

2. Choose your grade level.

3. Type in this book ID **142960025X** for age-appropriate sites. You may also browse subjects by clicking on letters, or by clicking on pictures and words.

4. Click on the **Fetch It** button.

FactHound will fetch the best sites for you!

23

Index

Word Count: 86
Grade: 1
Early-Intervention Level: 12

24